QUENCH THE THIRST

HERITAGE QUILT

M.D. Smith

QUENCH THE THIRST

HERITAGE QUILT

iUniverse books may be ordered through booksellers or by contacting:

iUniverse
1663 Liberty Drive
Bloomington, IN 47403
www.iuniverse.com
1-800-Authors (1-800-288-4677)

Because of the dynamic nature of the Internet, any web addresses or links contained in this book may have changed since publication and may no longer be valid. The views expressed in this work are solely those of the author and do not necessarily reflect the views of the publisher, and the publisher hereby disclaims any responsibility for them.

ISBN: 978-1-5320-9943-4 (sc)
ISBN: 978-1-5320-9944-1 (e)

Print information available on the last page.

iUniverse rev. date: 04/28/2020

Quench The Thirst

By: M.D. Smith

© 1994

Table of Contents

Dedication

This collection is dedicated to taking charge and embracing true joy in life.
So be adventurous, courageous, and energized.
Follow a positive path, embark on your journey
and
Quench The Thirst.

Author's Foreword
(Life Testimony – Pt.2)

This Part 2 of my life testimony continues, with some overlap, from Part 1 which is the Author's Foreword in my debut joint publication, In The Spirit: Poems Of My Thoughts • Roots Of My Heart. It exemplifies Galatians 6:9: "Let us not be weary in well doing; for in due season, you shall reap if you faint not" and the classic gospel song, "Let The Lord God Bless You Real Good" by Rev. James Cleveland.

At age 14, I was very clear that I was going to be an educator & entrepreneur after graduating from college, though I had multiple career interests that I considered and explored in civil rights law, management consulting, pediatrics, physical therapy, and sports management.

After graduating from my beloved college alma mater, I proceeded to find a place of employment in which I could use a combination of my natural talents and learned skills, especially any options to empower youth via education and compliment that with entrepreneurship. Frustratingly, I was unable to retain a job in the education field for more than (2) years. By 1990, I decided to be proactive in establishing myself as an entrepreneur. So, GOD inspired me with a vision to dba Mission Possible: Collaborative (MP:C) which is my consulting business that I've joyfully been doing part–time since Sept. 1990. Though elated to write my business plan for MP:C, I continued experiencing frustration with traditional employment. By 1994, 8 yrs. following college graduation, I had experienced (5) job changes.

Exasperated, I cried out to GOD one morning during my daily quiet time to ask: "Why?! Why am I going through this?! I'm clear about what I want to do as a profession. My loss of employment hasn't been due to poor job performance. So, why?!" The answer: Remember the prophetic word that your Nana Gerry shared with you (in Dec. 1985, one semester b4 your college graduation): "Granddaughter, you have great faith!" In retrospect, from that prophetic word 'til June 15, 2018, I realized that my Nana Gerry's prophetic word wasn't for that moment in Dec. 1985. It was meant to be a sustaining word for what I was going to go through upon graduating from college —a 30 year journey to realizing the deferred goal of of being joy-fully engaged in my purpose-full profession. June 15, 2018 was a breakthrough moment that fulfilled the prophetic word of my Nana Gerry and a follow–up prophetic word from my brotha, Rev. Hollis Cotton. Now, I'm in that purpose–fulll profession and evolving as GOD provides opportunity for me to do so. Along with the self–publication *of the 1ˢᵗ of (5) books in May 2018 — of which (4) comprise my creative writing collections and developing initiatives with my consulting business, MP:C, I can truly say that I am pleasantly "Exhausted From Being So Blessed" which is a 2ⁿᵈ dialogue that I wrote & presented prior to my 50ᵗʰ birthday in 2014.*

I give all thanks to The Power of The Holy Trinity for rewarding me as a direct result of adamant perseverance and "fighting the good fight of faith" which is granting me the blessing of "Living My Life Like It's Golden," one of my favorite songs by Jill Scott. ☺

Don't Be Empty In Heart or Mind

If you don't have "deep down" determination that comes from the heart,
then whatever you do will never stay with you;
When times are tough, you won't get through.

What you put in, you get back.
So learn from healthy habits and values,
and you'll majestically sprout, no doubt.

Don't be empty in mind;
strive to absorb all the good knowledge that you can.
So eventually, you can pass it on;
lend a helping hand.

Don't be empty in heart or mind.
Rather, develop fullness and thrive.

Get A Grip, Get Hip

Excuse me! There's nothin' wrong with people
who naturally act from the heart.
In fact, I'm one and get along just fine.
It irritates me when "certain people" believe
that we kind people are weak.
Wrong! Just the opposite, we are strong.

True character shines from the inside out.
It's not in material things, not in with whom you hang;
not in anything natural, it's a spiritual thang.

So as Shakespeare said, "To thine own self be true;"
in that go to the limit, be you.

Relationships

Relationships...whether across gender or within,
there is one major ingredient by which they are sustained —
2–way communication, simple and plain.

Why does it seem for some that they are doing all of the initiating?
If it isn't due to lack of care, desire, or love
then maybe it's due to a lack of prioritizing time?
Whatever the reason, we all have different styles and "comfort zones'
For giving and receiving. So, how do we appreciate and not take offense
to unequal reciprocation?
By being upfront in respectful communication,
we can come to mutual understanding.
For relationships to be healthy and long–lasting,
There must be an active consciousness of all parties involved;
and whenever there is discontent;
a favorable resolution should always be the desired resolve.

Return

A fortified standard was set for each of us, in place since our beginning.
However, we don't have to accept and/or continue
in the way that was paved.
Yet, we should have a sense of responsibility
to carry on culture, heritage, and history.
Our individual and collective survival is crucially linked
to not wavering, especially when difficult times press us against a wall.
We should not abandon, distance, or isolate
but rather uphold each other and stand tall.

So, let's return to exercising "The Golden Rule";
and value those in our "life circle" as a precious jewel.

Worthy To Follow

A wonderful privilege, to be had by anyone,
is to have a mentor — someone worthy to follow.
What's most important is choosing one you admire,
one who you can literally reach out and touch;
one who is near not far.
And for those who are asked or offer to be mentors,
it's a commitment to be taken seriously.
It's a position with potential of great influence;
it's one that requires integrity.
So, in your search, be "prayerfully wise";
and choose carefully someone who will give enriching advice.

Prayers I

Day:

Thank you Abba Father
for this new day.
Thank you for your continued provision.
Continue to order my steps and actions.
In the name of Jesus.
Amen!!! (3x)

Night:

Abba Father,
grant me peaceful and rejuvenating sleep this night.
Awake me to find that I, family, and friends are alive and alright.
In the name of Jesus.
Amen!!! (3x)

When All Is Said And Done

We all are given life for a purpose —
to live it in the best possible way.
By various means, we go about our business — everyday

We experience ups and downs,
times when we smile and times when we frown.
So in whatever state we are,
we must learn to be content by making a commitment.

Overcome negative with positive;
Know who you truly are, stand firm and you'll go far.
Press through your character and faith building tests;
and when it's all said and done,
your life will be a representation of "living challenges" won.

On The Edge

High Energy,
Conservative when necessary,
Adventurous when something new can be tried.
Like a surfer riding blue-green ocean waves
on the edge of the tide.

There's a time for balance;
there's a time for extreme;
a time to rise to challenges,
a time to retreat.

Find the courage and discipline it takes
to be active in all these ways.
And surely, your life will be anything but dull,
all your days.

So Close!

Have you ever had an experience when you've voiced, "So Close!"
—a favorite sports team playing their toughest rivalry,
yourself engaged in a game,
a test that you needed to pass,
or just having enough of something to last?
The list could go on
with situations that almost happen.
And someday your "so close!" experience
will find its way.
And you'll rejoice that you held onto the hope
that wishes do come true (in time),
for others and for you.

His Way or My Way?

"I Am The Way, The Truth, and The Life…' says The Living God.
So why do we have an itch to be anxious when we're waiting for Him —
that sign for what was just prayed?
It's our human nature kickin' up;
We think we need to make sure the answer isn't delayed.
Yet, it's not our role to play in our walk with Him.
We are to obey, submit, trust with joy;
He will come through, always without fail.
So, just sit back, relax, coast, and sail.
His Way not My Way;
I say, "yes, I say."

Blessed Be

(Song)

Verse:

Blessed Be The Rock of My Salvation
Blessed Be The Refuge for My Soul
Blessed Be The Rock of My Salvation
Oh!, Oh!, Blessed Be The Refuge for My Soul
(2x)

Bridge:

For you are My Strong Tower (3x)
And the righteous run in and are safe
(2x)

Repeat Verse

Fade Out

Waking Up

Our first taste of life — birth into this world.
And then toddler, youth, young adult, adult stages — we whirl.
What shapes us?:
our home, surrounding outside environment,
and some standards of life.
Yet, it's not until we start developing our individual, unique identities,
do we view The Light.
On through many scenarios,
we move toward our Rightful Places.
Whether fast or slow, just persevere
and finish your races.
So, if I'm slow (and have been)
in getting to where I'm supposed to be;
excuse me, support me with your prayers — please.

Feeling Helpless But Assured

Hangin' with a sista, we were rappin'
about what is and what should be.
She started talkin' about bein' free from a hazardous relationship;
The break was slow and hard.
She is being regularly bothered by "the one's physical appearances,"
phone calls, unsolicited slander.
"It's goin' to be o.k.," I encouraged her;
God is in control;
you don't have to wonder.
So, stay prayerful, take precaution,
and know you're under your Lord's protective cover.
Your freedom, joy unspeakable, and perfect peace
is in motion;
never to come undone.

The Truth About Christmas

Witnessing the birth of Christ, in Bethlehem at a lowly manger
under a bright, guiding star's light;
a light that drew (3) Kings and common folk bearing varied gifts
to celebrate that wondrous sight — this was the original Christmas.

So, noting its history; how it became commercialized
is a sad reality and mystery.
The mystery lies in the minds and hearts of those who don't acknowledge its origin
and forgot how to spell Christmas. It's not Xmas!
This is a grammatical fact that can't be dismissed.
It ain't right and it's disrespectful to cross out Christ from Christmas.
Then, pandemonium at stores, overspending, seasonal debt?
Wuz up with that???
Isn't there somewhere with some loved ones around whom you can get socially phat?

Coming together for quality time, enjoying special foods, listening & singing
the carols, renewing faith and hope —
this is primarily what celebrating Christmas is all about.
Then secondly, giving gifts: gifts of love, joy, peace, and practical/thoughtful/
desired ones; excited with anticipation in opening them and all the while having fun.
This is the complete picture of Christmas, for real.

So, if you're someone who knows the real deal, then do right —
live The Truth About Christmas,
share The Truth About Christmas,
celebrate The Truth About Christmas.

The Wrong Direction?

Awake and it's a new day
to live and strive to do right;
to face up to whether I'll stay or "take flight."
Searching for that straight & narrow path I'm suppose to be on.
In The Wrong Direction?
God, help me get to The Right Place.
What's that you say:
Oh, "watch & pray & seek your face?
O.K., got ya.
Thank you for hearing me and giving me that insight" to see.
You will always lead me away from The Wrong Direction,
and when necessary,
compel me with the quickness to flee.

Complete And New

Isn't it nice to have something new?
Something that you know you'll take good care of;
something that will last, through and through.
For me, it's not anything materialistic —
nothing that can be purchased at any price.
For me, what I treasure the most is my ever progressing,
personal relationship with Jesus Christ.
"Why," you say? Well, let me tell ya.
There have been times in my life,
in particular a seven-year trudge
of being caught up in a whirlwind of displacement.
And what Jesus did is sit me down in my spirit,
and said "It's time you got arrested."
I was not where I was suppose to be in Him,
and He said, "I have such, such great palns for you."
So, stop thinkin' and livin' like you have to hurry and do, do, do.
Instead, pace yourself, seek Me for the answers —
and I'll bring you through.
"Yes, indeed!!!," I replied excitingly.
I had finally caught hold of the true meaning of "wait."
And now, on My Right Path,
I'm thriving — success in abundance is my fate.

Beyond Imagination

Can you fathom having your desires, dreams, and special interests
all together — enjoying them at the same time?
Well, I have experienced the feeling.
And if at least one time in life, you may say but then realize,
"No, I'm not dreaming."

It's really for real, secure and cuddled and secure
like a kryptonite lock on a bicycle's wheels.
Unspeakable joy, I just can't contain;
I'm living every second of every moment;
my happiness, health, and prosperity will remain.

Magic Moments

In anything you do, you hope to work in sync.
'Til then, there is an adjustment period by which we must join
"the content tools" (to depend on each tool doing its part) —
all of them we must use.
On a sports team, it's teamwork, "game play flow;"
In relationships and living, it's sensitivity, consideration,
honesty, and communication.
And when the time is right, Divine Intervention steps in and with
pure grace and tenderness puts everything in its place.
I'm so glad for "The Magic,"
'cause my source is My Father above.
And in "The Magic" is evident His love.

A Year of Jubilee

Before New Year's Day 1995 rolled around, A Year of Jubilee had begun —
the joy was like hearing a favorite song's sound.
But shortly, thereafter came two tests to bear;
they came hard and strong, piercing my heart with a "spiritual spear."
Temporarily, I was down in spirit and hurt to the core, but then The Lord reminded me
that great blessings hardly ever come without a serious fight.
So, He said, "Gear up with My Whole Armour
and prepare to battle and send the enemy to flight."
Many times, in personal battles, you have to stand your ground alone;
No one nearby to give counsel, pray, and/or cover your back.
So, all the more you must seek and trust The Lord for a plan with tact.
'Cause truly, the enemy uses tact: he's sneaky, pitifully shameless, and the father of lies.
So focus in The Spirit, use to the hilt, your supernatural eyes.
The only way to keep the ground you've gained
is to stay before The Lord, daily with prayer.
Continue to seek His guidance, cherish your blessings and be a blessing;
and all your concerns cast upon Him, for He cares.

A Birthday Poem

Birthdays are a great time to reflect as well as celebrate;
to be thankful for living another year,
to hopefully look forward to starting the new one with cheer.

May God continue to keep you steady and ready;
Keep striving and thriving,
Be blessed and eliminate being stressed.

Peace & Love

Growth Ahead

A native in the native land;
comfortable, loving life so grand.
Then comes a swift change in mind;
really has been coming but in its own sweet time.
Pondering and shortly realize:
Yes, it's time to move on, gotta jet toward what's ahead;
Can't deny what my spirit needs to be fed.
No doubt about it, The Call is from Above;
Excited about the dawning of a new stage —
escorted by pure love.
So, receive with care, humility, and wisdom, your tools for growth ahead;
and surely, your steps to success will be divinely led.

Carpe Diem!
("Seize The Day")

Hey, Hey, it's today!!!;
make the most of your precious time —
balance time for business and recreational/social play.
Carpe Diem is all about "seizing the day" —
being as productive and pleasantly fulfilled as possible.
Take hold of that realm and "rock it!"
Shine bright and keep your "life light" lit.
Go for what is beyond your reach,
and you'll experience something amazing that maybe one day you can teach.
In one of my favorite all–time movies, Dead Poets Society,
there's an invaluable life lesson taught by the late great Robin Williams —
'follow your heart and do your passions —Carpe Diem ("Seize The Day").
Don't let any time pass by without enjoying each moment of each day in your life.
Don't let anyone cause you strife;
rather live your life to its maximum potential and do your best to always do right.

Carpe Diem — "Seize the Day;"
"do you" in your own unique way.

Fellowship Festival

Togetherness: Celebrations… Holidays…Special Occasions…Weekends…
Bein' with your "hang out crew",
lookin' to be adventurous, try something new.
It's the place to be when you're feeling blue;
alone, don't know what to do.
Drum up a fellowship festival —
spontaneity with some coordination creates it.
Dance, Eat, Talk,
Whatever your position, the goal is to be refreshed,
So, do it as needed;
and the result will show —social interaction, completed.

Vacation From The City

A dear sista and fellow college alumna offered to me a simple, yet very pleasant gift —
An opportunity to housesit, escape the hubbub of the city, be refreshed,
experience an "energy lift."
I accepted and proceeded to have a good time in solace;
but with a void in hangin' out with family for the holiday weekend.
So, I got together with a few friends;
and everyone's presence brought an air of delight to the solace of the entire stay.
It's always different to do something other than the usual,
and in this case, it was also a pleasant & enjoyable time
purely sublime.

My Love For Life

The Lord God was and still is the #1 love of my life.
And then you came along —gentle, honest, open to receive
someone I could love strong.
We started to spend quality time together —sharing, laughing, loving the courtship.
And we realized that we both felt giggly every time we journeyed on a "social trip."

What's next as we take it one day at a time?
Do we sense that we're moving closer to saying,
"I'm so glad that you're mine!"
Yes! The feeling is mutual;
We desire to be One.
So, let's pledge for eternity for it to be done.

"Straight Up" Honest

Coming clean, coming clean —clean away from the past.
Going forward toward my destined place —
building a positive legacy, somethin' that will last.
So hard sometimes, a constant process of living God's Way;
Yet, truly, "Obedience is better than sacrifice", His Way pays.
Discipline and Faith; with His strength, they must be daily used;
and the blessings will come in orchestration, a thrilling sensation.

So, just stay in the mode of "straight up" honest.
No matter how difficult,
God will guide you through;
Keep your spirit right and enjoy life.

It's All Good

When life is up, when life is down;
"it's all good" 'cause God's around.
Surrounded by His grace, mercy, and power;
He continues to open my eyes —
Showing me, here and there, a wonderful surprise.
Ain't gonna give up,
Ain't gonna give in;
No matter what I'm in The Race to win.
Take a chance and gain assurance, that in the end, "it's all good."
Be strong and be of good courage like ya should.

Ode To My Dad

Handsome and tall, light cream–skinned with hazel color eyes;
emotional pain and internal trauma became his demise.
Given all that he faced, he ran his "life race" well;
And time took its course and its story it did tell.

Together with our family for 25 years;
and then illness intensified, brought us to tears.
He was gentle, generous, caring, kind, and loving;
but sadly, all that got lost —
his actions 'til the end resulted in an irreversible cost.

Dad, I miss you so much!!!
I wish life could've been better for you.
So, 'til next we connect, just know I'll always love you.
XOXOXO

My Favorite Great American Heroes

They share in common: cultural heritage, firm convictions, ethics and values —
all (working together) in motion at the same time
to improve the quality of life for all humankind.
My top five: Harriet Tubman, Mary McLeod Bethune, Ida B. Wells,
MLK, Jr., and Malcolm X.
They were all great in using their brilliance,
their minds they did flex.
There are so many more that could be named here in these lines;
But for you to have your top 5, you only must seek and find.
So to all our true great American heroes,
Let us never forget their courage and sacrifices.
Let us rather applaud, uphold, pass on their memory throughout the generations.
Remember: 365, not just the holidays, embrace them in celebrations.

Through The Storm

The year was 1986, the occasion — college graduation;
and when the ceremony was over,
it was now time to face "what's next?"
Onward to professional basketball,
I looked forward to making my mark —standing tall.
Uh, but it wasn't the right timing for KFUM–Uppsala (SWEDEN) to have me,
so only for a half season did I stay.
Yet, I returned home, still ready and desiring to play.
United States Basketball League (USBL) and intramural leagues,
pick–up games here & there, working in a traditional career;
Time passed and the routine began to wear.
Too many unexpected transitions,
this isn't what I envisioned to be the "road to success."
However, God impressed upon me, at my peak of frustration,
This is the road, oh yes!
This storm's fierce persistence confirmed; it was a tiered steppingstone.
Each year, bringing me closer to my destiny —
as I endured the testing of my faith and learned to wait.
So, the "storm" has finally subsided and the sun is shining brightly in my life.
I look forward to the path before me,
going on with an attitude of victory.

No Matter What

Living life on its terms —it's not always easy, it's not always comfortable;
but no matter what,
we have to work through with the knowledge we got.

A major key is learning from past mistakes
and actively applying the lessons, whatever it takes.
For me, I struggle sometimes;
but no matter what, I keep pressin.'
Determined to be holistically well,
encourage others with a testimony to tell.

As this goal is put to the test,
I grab hold to my Help and believe The Best.
I am sure there will be other times ahead that I'll miss the mark.
But no matter what, I'm gonna come to the light, not stay in the dark.
So, no matter what people say or think about me —
I'm a spirit in progress —in God's hands, I'm free.

Reflection

Looking in the bathroom mirror —sitting with my feelings and thoughts;
evaluating the year gone by, these are my means of reflection.
In the silence of the moments, I wait to hear from within:
What needs to change? What can be improved?
What action must I take? In what way must I move?
There's been much that has happened;
there are issues to address.
The support is available;
time to step up and pro–gress.
Reflection —to search, to find; to live at peace in mind;
Reflection —it's healthy;
for me, it's a wholesome connection.

P.R.I.D.E. & E.G.O.

P.R.I.D.E. — Practicing Raw Ill Destructive Energy & E.G.O. (Easin' God Out)
are two insidious behaviors which function hand–in–hand.
P.R.I.D.E. feeds E.G.O. and E.G.O feeds P.R.I.D.E.;
it's a vicious, negative cycle, don't ya know?
Get up the courage and say to these (2): Gotta Go, Gotta Go!!!.
Hit the exit door and don't ever come back no more.
When they knock or try to creep back in, don't let them overpower and win.
They love a body that will keep 'em puffed up and riding high.
Be always "on point" — say to them "you can't reside here, takin' me down.

I & God are in charge;
So you better act like ya know and just blow — like the wind.
Your reign is history and no it ain't no mystery.
You are air to me;
so "bounce," "beat it" and permanently stay away.
'Cause never with God's help, will you lead me astray.

Be Out!!!

Let It Go, Let It Flow

Can't hide behind the masks of facial pretense;
Gotta be real, rather than right; be flexible not tight.
Unconsciously, the layers of facades can stack themselves — thick;
but when we realize this just can't be,
we must peel away, discard, and restart with the original part.
No more time can be wasted exercising the alter egos.
Time to remember and get back to the identity that's true;
good for me, good for you.
Gotta get into that rhythm, in the groove of "for real;"
want to claim my stake —function on my pure appeal.
Like being "in that zone" on the basketball court;
lettin' it go, lettin' it flow.
Destination —arrival will manifest itself at the time that is best.
So, let it go, let it flow;
prepare to reap what you sow.

When You're Ready

LORD, LORD — When You're Ready to move by Your Spirit,
nothing can hold it back.
When You're Ready to do something in us and through us,
it's always right on time;
it's sweetness — sublime.
When You're Ready, you'll shake Heaven and Earth;
the ripple effect lingers long & strong and it finally hits us.

What will my decision be?
Will I heed to the signposts clearly marking the way
or will I not be obedient nor surrender and be led astray?
I don't know about you, but I'm down for choice #1;
and I'll only follow through successfully if my eyes are fixed on The Son.

When You're Ready, LORD,
Your Word goes forth and doesn't return void.
When You're Ready, LORD,
healing is released, blessings flow,
and all that is not of you rears its face
and it can't hang, so it leaves the place.

The place is now full with "the fruit of The Spirit:
love, joy, peace, patience, kindness, goodness, faithfulness, gentleness, and self–control.
It's been available for you to tap into all along,
you just had to come to realize, now you know.

Go on with that power from on high, accompanied by unspeakable joy —
for when The LORD is ready to make dat move, prepare to be amazed;
and walk on a different plane, remembering to give Him all da praise.

Liftin' Him Up

Raise the roof!, Raise the roof!;
ain't enough room to keep this on the inside.
Full to capacity, the presence of Him is splitting the seams wide.
When we honor Him, ourselves, and others, He gets lifted up high.
Where He dwells apart and within us, it's limitless as is the sky.

If all the voices of the world belonging to Him rang out in one accord,
It wouldn't be enough to say how wonderful and great, thou art oh Lord!!!
Praise, honor, and glory; you deserve it all.
Your people can give it with authority;
knowing in all things, you're The One to call.

My desire is to be meek
so that I can continue to be empowered — day by day, week to week.
Yes, yes, yes, as often as possible, I'll be liftin' Him up!!! —
constantly emptying out and open for Him to fill "my cup."

Diamonds In The Rough

Considered unruly, misunderstood, a hidden treasure;
seeking to find that certain pleasure.
Wanting to shine;
hopin' to get that chance, sooner rather than later in time.
Just need some polish to spiff up and stand out;
just need that one factor to bring it about, no doubt.
I'm custom designed by The Creator, I'm a diamond in the rough.
Grant me some sandin' so I can be smooth & soft, not jagged & tough.
Hardest of all the precious gems,
I'm gonna be one of them.
Through shaping and molding and enduring the immense heat;
I'll become solid from the core to the surface, from my head to my feet.

What a glorious day it's gonna be when my countenance glows, oh so;
I'll be positioned to stand firm and grow;
and help others be the same — bright as the brightest flame.

Faith Pedal To The Medal

It was the challenge of my lifetime, thus far.

No time to forget the answer to: Remember whose you are?

The intersection of my crossroads bore two definitive choices:

Do I lose my courage to fight; or plan to realize victory

and after Rejoice! Rejoice! Rejoice!?

I chose the latter 'cause I've crossed over to "the greener side" several times before.

All I needed was a special portion of faith and I would overcome once more.

As a fuel pedal to the medal in an automobile starts it racing;

so did my heart and my faith keep me from wavering.

The scenario appeared dismal; and at times hope seemed to be lost.

But, My GOD spurred me on and His resounding voice gently whispered:

"You're going to make it; hope isn't lost."

And the complementing affirmation shined clear:

Sheer determination and divine will fully joined to complete 'The Big Picture."

Just wade in the joy of knowin' that it won't be long

'til those "hangin' in the balance' blessings start flowin'.

How marvelous it is —"all things work together for the good…;"

I'm living proof,

and my willing obligation is to reproduce my record, let it take root.

Just All–Around Beautiful

Something just right with that first encounter;
a mutual acquaintance introduced us and as I listened, I wondered:
What is it that's given me this instant connection?
There was tone, enthusiasm, genuineness, warmth, and passion.
The after–effect seemed to linger in the air; present itself to be everlasting.
We persisted to meet; but not until it was the right time.
We sat face–to–face in a jazzy, sophisticated, festive place.
The attention was gradually magnetic.
As we got our conversation on, we vibed and it was eclectic.
Strikingly solid in every way: emotionally, intellectually, socially, and spiritually,
I believe this righteous one is in my life to stay.
A friendship in the making is where our roads will culminate.
Just all–around beautiful — the value of coming together will appreciate.

Quality Relations

Him then Her.
He eased into my life as a neighbor first then evolved into a friendly companion,
a "social quench of thirst."
She finally had clearance in her schedule and a rendezvous lasted for (4) days.
All that she gave left me in a pleasant daze.
These (2) were firmly grounded in their faith and "on fire."
Enjoying our enriching interaction,
keeping focus on what we're building.
To have them in my life so alive and vibrantly,
it's refreshingly amazing; I'm content and my heart is elated.
What will be the miracle of the co—existence of these two as it relates to me?
God knows and it will be as it should be.

Bonding Ties

Family & friends, friends & family; to me the two are interchangeable.
Building relations, producing creations, foundations laid,
creating the next generation's pathway.
It is so important not to take for granted the time we have on this Earth.
Rather, we need to stay in regular communication and avoid stagnation; go forth.

Why wait 'til a crisis or tragedy arises before "linking up" with those most dear to us?
Treat your bonding ties with more respect;
and more exuberance, you can expect.
When locking the ties that are meant to bind, adhere to "the tried and true":
Let GOD be the Guide of it all;
so in the end, everyone raises their conscious contact —
agreeing that staying in touch is the pact.

The Next Level: Raising The Standard

Life is about choices; life is about process and progress —
one step / one moment at a time.
Eventually, the stage evolves when you're able to say,
"all in my life is wonderfully fine."
What a feeling, what a position to be in!
The toiling, the pressing, the stretching has wound down;
let the hallelujah chorus sing loud.
Really can't thoroughly express the unspeakable joy that reverberates in my soul;
enjoying this next level has only come via exercising some deep discipline and self–control.
The Next Level: Raising The Standard —
if ya gonna keep growing, aging like a fine wine;
then your priority must be holding fast to wholesome principles —
continually applying them in line.

No Compromise

When you're grounded in a set of ethical, moral, and spiritual principles,
there's just no wavering about certain subjects,
the passing prodding, I must reject.
Unconditional feelings are to remain firm and translate into rules that you stand by.
No influence, regardless of its form, should force your beliefs/principles
to be tossed to the wayside.
"Stand for something or you'll fall for anything" — the saying goes;
Have love and respect enough for yourself that anyone who truly cares about you knows.

Our world, our society, our neighborhoods need folk of all ages
to declare a "reclaim pure values & lifestyles war."
It's time to turn away, totally, from the negative;
and with the positive, settle "The Score."

Are Ya Feeling It?!

Feelings have a diversity of faces,
they are ever–present for those in tuned to then in many places.
What really dictates how you really feel?
Is it circumstances which carry a fraction of drama or is it your intuitive —
the core of your spirit where lies the real?
Whether it's just exuberant joy for relishing a simple or unexpected pleasure
or sadness/sorrow/anger for injustices or an event turned unfair;
are ya feeling it?! Is it something you care to share?
Emotional, Intellectual, Spiritual, Therapeutic —
these are the "heavy weights" of the "feelings classes."
As you confront and sift through, eventually serenity will embrace you.
To feel what is beyond what you can think or imagine,
no phrase can capture the full essence.
Ya just have to be there, have to feel its presence.

Being There

Yo, here's the scenario:
Have you ever been there for someone or vice versa?
It's those deep, emotionally hard times when it counts the most;
do you have what it takes to comfort, nurture, provide some support?
True colors shining through;
you were there for me; I'll be there for you.
It doesn't take anything grand or magical to just be there;
just be available and lend a listening ear.
Offer your body to lean on, your resources to share.
At times, it's about self–sacrifice — that act of being "super nice."
Appreciated beyond words and never forgotten as a selfless deed,
just being there is a wonderful way to meet someone's need.

Follow Your Dreams

Yours, original, and boasting with its own kind of fanfare —
You hold on tight and map out a plan;
with each step, you increase your confidence to "Yes, I can."
Whatever the effort,
you keep on takin' your energy to higher heights.
There's no stoppin' ya when you're on a roll.
Ya shootin' for that star,
steeped deep in motivation and striving from the depths of your soul.
And finally, the day comes when it all comes together and you're face-to-face;
you've weathered the storms and now you're in your refined form.
If you build up a strong, solid inner belief
and don't allow anything or anyone to deter you;
your trek to live your dream(s) will no longer appear to seem —
it will be.

Gratitude Speaks For Itself

Never assuming, taking advantage of or for granted
the miracles that are in front of my eyes.
To see the root of my good fortune, I must view it from the supernatural side.
Have to locate and focus in on where my gratitude lies.
Is it positioned to speak for itself or is it hangin' out in a corner or on a shelf?

Gratitude — being grateful, embracing bein' truly humbled.
This is what this action word means to me.
If you sincerely have it, it exudes without any assistance.
If you yearn to show it, your attempts to exchange will be persistent.
You will not be able to rest with an unfinished "thank you transaction,"
your spirit & soul, stirred 'til you have released to satisfaction.

Gratitude Speaks For Itself —
when you've received your help, and you handle this gem
with awestruck command.

Identify • Accept • Process •Move On

In my opinion, there are (4) principles
that are the "how to guide" to confronting shortcomings.
They are also the tools to ongoing comprehension
of what is in & out of your control.
As individuals, we are only responsible for what we say,
what we do, how we interact and sort through our "life facts."

Identify — Who am I?,
good & bad habits, problems & solutions.
Accept — me for who I am,
the things I cannot change (out of my control),
my goal to self–improve, go to higher plains.
Process — the root, the true nature of my feelings,
healthy contact with my "people dealings;"
the solutions to my problems/hang–ups,
faith and support may not be enough.
Move On — identified, accepted, processed, now it's time to move on.
This is not to say, at this point, that all fear or resistance or denial is all gone.
No, this is just a part of life's journey where you don't get stuck,
bogged down in the mire and muck.
Rather, you hit head on
all that you are, all that you have, where you are and where you're going;
and the praise report will be the fruition of staying in the knowing.

Abundance

It's a wealth that's beyond calculated measure;
priceless, an eternal treasure.
What it is —
it's the gift of a loving people network: family, friends, positive–minded acquaintances.
Taken in the beauty of sharing each other's company;
laughing, counting our blessings one by one, thanking GOD for all He does and has done.
Consoling in times of sorrow/stress;
reaching for that which will endear us through life's mess.
Havin' good times/fun times in all its forms;
unconditional joy, love, and giving is to be the norm.
We all need to search and find this kind of limitless abundance.
It is what GOD wants for us (and what we should want, too) —
life full of abounding abundance and minimal fuss.

Revelations At Hand

With every "learned something new,"
there is an increase in my knowledge bank.
I add to my perspective;
it widens and my GOD, I thank.
As I am permitted to live,
each period bears an excitement to the revelations at hand.
Common Sense & Biblical Principles —
I have a better grasp and they're becoming easier to understand.
I'm seein' more enlightenment in my revelations at hand.
The simple delights, oh my, oh my!
They're such that they set me off to fly, to wanna be flyin' high.
I'll be livin' large as they unfold — my revelations at hand.
I'll continually harvest the "crops" as I heed to Your Every Command.
Bring 'em on, bring 'em on; my Revelations At Hand.

Prayers II

(i)

"LORD, please grant me the privilege of fulfilling my purpose on this Earth
with the talents in my DNA.
I believe and pray that you will not take me to eternal life
before my appointed time.
And in laying the foundation of my next generation,
you'll bless it to be a sweet sensation.

(ii)

"Your Promises are so true, oh LORD;
and I pray to see them all come to pass.
"You cannot fail to come through with 'the goods.'"
So, I'll be standing with open arms to receive what I should.

Heritage Quilt
(A Collection of Poetry & Essays)
By: M.D. Smith

© 1999

Table of Contents

Heritage Quilt

None of us are ever really alone in our life on this Earth.
Why? 'Cause we are a member of a family from birth.

If you're among those who have had their back covered by loved ones,
what a great advantage you're at, to be so rich like that.
As a masterfully woven fabric will wear forever,
so does a finely developed support system —
especially one established with the center being Him.

Heritage Quilt — in addition to the physical factors,
compliment it with what the spiritual can build.

Unity vs. Division

Wuz up with this "I got mine, you get yours" mentality
amongst certain people of color??
I can't fathom how someone of color who is half–way conscious
of their race's history can forget??
It's unconscionable to me how the oppression, the racism, the tokenism,
and the superior/inferior complex (Bell Curve Theory) can be absent
from the mind of an ancestral descendant whose life was subtly difficult
due to these conditions.
If you are in a position to help/lift others of your kind
to where they are purposed to be, The Bible says you should do it —
Proverbs 3:27 (KJV)—
"Withhold not good from them to whom it is due,
when it's in the power of thine hand to do it."

So, when as a collective race is unity vs. division gonna become a reality again?
'Cause we once had this concept down —
when it was survival for all during those almost (400) years of slavery.
The goal was to leave no one behind to the cruelty of slavery's existence.
What makes headin' into the New Millenium any different than the 1500s?
Slavery just has a different look —
Instead of chains, shackles, plantations, and controlled living environments,
there are subliminal messages of genocide
which are played out in race–on–race crimes, the devastating effects of drugs,
miseducation of your true being/lineage.

See, when you got knowledge — that no one can take away
and you're securely confident in what ya know,
then you break the cycle of "the slave mentality"
and you regain the true essence of who you are.
Who are you? Descendants of royalty — kings & queens;
Ya need to get hip and step up on "the corrected scene."

How do ya find your "corrected scene?
You begin with re–educating yourself (and anyone you can in your social circle).
Read some books, talk with your elders in your family & community,
research your family tree;
come out of prison and set yourself, and whoever else needs to be, free.

Stress—Free

Some objectives can be accomplished almost immediately,
while others can't hurried/expedited.
It is the second of these objectives which I will address here.
These tend to be "the long—term, benefit ones" which we need/want instantly.
But the time is not yet near.
We can't control, the uncontrollable; expect the unexpected;
Do more than the best of our current ability.
When these facts are kept upfront then we be literally stress—free.
Why get all caught up in an emotional and /or mental tizzy?
Your only result will be you'll spin yourself dizzy.

Life is too short to drum up unnecessary, negative vibes.
So, concentrate only on that which is important and forget all the jive.
Stress—Free, Stress—Free —
that's how I practice to live every moment of my existence.
Stress— Free, Stress—Free,
don't you wanna be?!

What Do You Really See?

Are your eyes clear to see what it is really goin' on?
What do you really see when you gaze upon a homeless person? —
do you think "there's a lazy bum repeating: "Spare Change, Spare Change"
or someone who was once like you but has fallen on hardship?

What do you really see in someone who is physically or mentally challenged?
Do you cringe at the deformity / the abnormalness?
or do you applaud the courage that many have to spur on despite their disability?

What do you really see when you acknowledge that someone you know
has a shortcoming/shortcomings which can be irritable?
Do you cut off your relationship with them and maintain a closed mind
about how & who they are or do you watch & observe, wishing for a healthy change,
so with you, they're no longer estranged?

Don't look at the surface of any circumstance or person
to define what you really see.
Take your insight to the depth of substance, and what you find that you should believe.

Not By Invitation: Ya Can't Come In!

Why (are) ya cramping my style?;
tryin' to come in uninvited and stay a while.
Puhleez!!! You have some gaul, attempting to interrupt my peace;
so if you don't leave by my request,
then I'm gonna have to take authority and your "bogart self" arrest.
I rebuke you in the name of Jesus;
So get to steppin' — move your slew feet.
In the name of Jesus, you can't stand in His Presence;
'cause you're a foe, always with the agony of defeat.
Let me ensure that you go back to where you belong, swiftly.
Here's my anointing oil to cover me in my refuge space,
and anywhere else to protect me from your evil fate.
Now, I've assured ya can't hang out here and impose on me any kind of strife.
To all who hear, I say, get your soul & spirit aligned with The Living God (Yehovah)
and then you'll have a life.

Anchored In Balance

Affirmation & Confirmation —
receiving them through various situations.
My "journey quest" to be thoroughly even–balanced is grounded in continual chances.
Open doors to get it right this time around;
don't you do anything to put me down.
I'm givin' my best concentration for where I'm at;
don't assume I'll always be like that.
As you wish to be known for who you really are;
grant me the same and watch me go far.
If you sincerely care about my welfare
then cheer me on in my "journey quest";
to be anchored in balance, I'm gonna be My Best.

Basking In The Unspeakable

Too awesome, I just can't tell you the fullness of what I am feeling.
What I can tell ya is it's the simplicity of wrappin' myself around
all that is pure, peaceable, gentle, and oooh sooo good!

It's a state of mind & being that everyone deserves, feelin' the way ya should.
It's all that is enriching, positive, growth—based, inspiring, and fulfilling.
My joy I just can't contain; it's continually spilling.

The smile on my face, side—to—side wide;
The laughter and over exuberant elation is evident from every side.
If I had to sum up where I'm at in my life: I can assuredly say:
"I've been through some heavy situations, but now I've entered in.
I'm basking in the unspeakable, don't you wanna join in?

It's Just The Way It Is

Raw & Unflawed, it's what's termed "The Real Deal."
No falsehood, no hang ups — it's what can't be altered or whisked away;
it's all that has to be just the way it is.
We have all had or will have instances where we're staring at the core,
the root and nothing can transform its image.
The circumstances, situation, person — it's just the way it is.
Don't try to fix what ain't broken, and don't cross the boundary of
forcing something or someone to be;
you aren't suppose to be exercising that kind of authority.
Remember, your place;
give that whatever "it' is, space.
Move to give the correct type of support;
and don't get in "the divine way" and the perfect plan, thwart.
Ya gotta be mindful, get to it bein' second nature in all of your biz;
there are just some realities that it's just the way it is.

Ego Trippin' After Dark

Gotta give props to my sistuh that coined the term "Ego Trippin" —
Nikki Giovanni, she's so fierce.
So much so that that famous poem's words to the mind, pierce.
It's a reminder that we people of African descent are so wealthy, beyond
compare. What's lacking is our consciousness, to this fact, bein' aware.

It's wack, without tact, matter of fact — a shame.
We're <u>too independent</u> and should not project, no one but ourselves to blame.
Some need to stop floppin' & flippin'; half-steppin, stop trippin'.
Too much valuable time is bein' wasted on petty, foolish nonsense.

Show yourself real and forego all the pretense.
Ego Trippin' After Dark — contribute to us makin' our mark;
Don't be bound by the illness, the stereotypes of the past;
Take action to do something that will last.

Chillin' Skillz: Do Ya Got Some?

Chillin', Relaxin', Maxin'—is what to do when not on the job.
It's the way to unwind, rest your mind, get wit' some calm time.
Sample Examples ; Do That ; Kickin' Back —
in these moments, you can be slack.
No Deadlines —listen to your favorite songs in multiple rewinds.
A favorite pastime : classic or other type of film views,
good conversation with a "G", exchanging some enriching news.
Fragrance from a walk in a countryside, park, or public garden;
seein' some radiant sights —by day, sun shining; by night, sky lights.
If ya dig deep in open–mindedness,
there's no ceiling on the flava of your "chillin' skillz breaks."
Find and roll with 'em, learn 'em if you don't got 'em.
They'll be health to your bones and nourishment for your soul.
Chillin' Skillz —ya gots to have 'em for your wellness sake;
true dat, relax in control.

Territory : Unchartered

Not a typical 1st time experience — no anxiety, no nervousness, no issues,
no emotional roadblocks, n high expectations.
Just asked a couple of questions, walked away with the answers,
found my seat again and began takin' in the room.
Sat with brewing anticipation for the Poetry Slam to start soon;
my turn came, stepped up to the mic —
delivered my read with calm, confident ease.
Wasn't thinkin' about the prizes, just wanted to have fun;
and after listening and applauding to the end, my fun I had done.

For me, art is meant to be observed, interpreted, and appreciated for self.
It's not to be analyzed, critiqued, and scored;
It needs to be valued organically for its wealth.
The experience was o.k.—in fact, educational, fun, and insightful.
I tell ya, though, my preference is being strictly down with open mic venues
and the "publishing halls."
It's where I've always felt most alive and free-spirited, where I "rock on."

Never Been Here Before

Doin' responsibility — taught it and learned it well.
Yet, I'm facing a situation that has me in a bind.
So, I had to go to meditation and prayer and get hook on some peace of mind.
I had to reach out for help to resolve this one;
So I laid out the issue with two friends and they were positioned to label my dilemma,
"call it done."
For a fleeting moment, this situation caused me uneasiness and uncomfortability,
but not at any juncture did fear set in.
'Cause My GOD always meets my needs right on time,
even if it is in the final hour.
He's just "on point" in every flex of His power.
Once again, I gained assurance that "nothing is impossible with GOD
and all things work together for good to them that love Him."
So for any more of those, "Never Been There Befores,"
I got the know how to prod through and nestle faith anew.

Just Plain Fun

Your life's memory leaves behind an inheritance of genuineness, kindness,
and just plain fun;
included in that inheritance, you also gave birth and raised well
your (4) daughters and (3) sons.
Whenever I think of you, it brings a smile to my face.
Your warmth, faith, strength, constant encouragement, and motherly advice,
I always appreciated and embraced.
What I'll remember distinctly about you is your voice and laughter,
all those now treasured Thanksgiving/ Christmas /New Year's visits
to your house and the lingering good feelings, after.
I also will never forget the moments we had to converse one-to-one;
and one particular one we had about persevering through life's ups & downs.
You gave me a word that I'll always hold onto —
just like my mother continues to give to me.
I can't believe you're gone, it just came too early for me;
but despite the deep sadness, I have great joy
'cause I know you're back with The Lord now, free.
Keep an eye out for my dad and when you see him,
tell him I miss & love him so.
And 'til we meet again in eternal life; your life's memory, I'll never let go.

Breathin' Room

Get Back! Step Off! Why are you workin' my last nerve?!
I already told you (and have repeated myself) that the situation is under control.
So, why aren't you payin' attention and why are you respondin' with assumptions
and pessimism?
Can't you just give it a break?
Stop tryin' to take my mind and emotions over the "hot coals rake."
It's petty what you're keepin' in front of me.
Open your ears, hear me: you need to exhibit some understanding, please, please.
Come off of "the control/crackin' the whip trip" and get intuned with the realities of life
(especially the unannounced), get a grip.
I know I got it straight; but for you, you have to sit and wait.
So do that and quit puttin' out unnecessary petty communication.
Don't you have something of higher priority?
Come to common sense and give the process and me a fair chance.
Let's be logical in dealing with this affair;
'cause I got rights to exercise and I'll use 'em to fight, I swear.
So, why don't you just do the compassionate thing without compromising yourself.
Give yourself some breathin' room and scrap all the junk;
Put it forever away 'cause it's worthless, anyway.

The Least Is Much

Luke 16:10 — *"He that is faithful in that which is least is faithful also in much."*

Lord, you know just how much I can bear; so much
so that you give me instruction simply,
showing how deep you care.
The depth of life isn't about what's gained in material wealth.
In fact, You remind me that what's more important is the status of my spirit & soul
—keeping You first and leavin' the reigns of my life in your control.
You always have a way of keeping life simple and revealing progress,
step–by–step.
Takin' the work–at–it route" is the way to go;
I love when I wallow in this simplicity, just "goin' with the flow."

Faithful, even when I fall short because I'm human,
You truly operate in grace and mercy.
You are the model for me to study, apply, and strengthen my "faith-full exercises"
and all that is the fruit of Your Spirit.
When I meditate on what my faithfulness perfected will looks like,
It's powerful and its rewards will have no limits.

Thank you, Lord for spoonfeeding me with the way to firmly stand and declare:
"I am faithful!!!"
You spark me to strive with focus —
for that and all you teach me, I'm forever grateful.

My Connection To Where History Began

AFRICA (aka "The Motherland") —
There is so much that comes to mind
about the continent that's the richest in diamond mines.
The aesthetic beauty of the landscape isglorious, especially near all the seaports
and rural mountainous areas.
The fashion wear, the culinary fare; the amazin' extended family networks,
the solidarity through the era of resistance — stamina enhanced by insistence.

Thus far, I have only had indirect insight to all that comprises the 54 countries.
However, my heart and missions direction is going to take me directly there
and excitingly result in creating wonder-full memories to share.
The country most attached to my deep love for "the
sensation of civilization" is South Africa.

Having delved diversely into African–African Studies (my 2ⁿᵈ major in college
and ongoing learning), I was moved to a motivation like never before,
to give of myself in any way to forward The Movement
in the areas of Education, Training, and Economic Development.
I am adamantly dedicated to making a contribution of benefit to the New South Africa.
The New South Africa — a democracy in evolving development,
led by the late President Nelson Mandela.
How fitting it was for him to lead the charge to bring South Africa
into its rightful position out of the era of apartheid.
Empowerment & Equality — these primary concepts
needed to come to full manifestation.
In divine time, coupled with diligent footwork, The New South Africa
will enter into its destination.
I look forward to being amongst the number
that will be able to claim a piece of that glorious day.
'Til then, it's all gonna be about focusing on the tasks at hand.
Like Malcolm X advocated "by any means necessary,"
I'll be down with any solid win–win agenda plan.

The Real Beauty

Such dignity &grace,
complimented by a body in progress and a beautiful face.
When it all arrives, it enriches the places
where it fills the spaces.
It's not what's on the outer appearance,
which is magnificent all by itself.
Rather, what really is the true essence is what's on the inner —that's def.
Dat inner though is a work-in-progress,
developing to be fine-tuned.
And when it gets to be super sharp, the growth will spread even
and in every area, make room.
Make room to be increasingly transparent, humble, in touch with your feelings
(especially the painful ones).
The life of that growing inner self molds deeper & deeper with that of the Son.
This is a picture of Real Beauty —
striving to be ; hungering to evolve, doing the footwork, then waiting to see;
excited with anticipation of what can actually be The Real Beauty.
Wow, you're so beauti-full!!!

Show Then Tell

The adage "Action Speaks Louder Than Words" —
you've adopted this as your life's philosophy;
but in a rewritten phrase, this is your ideology —
Show Then Tell."
And truly, you excel in consistently exhibiting through & through,
'cause you're so spirit-led in everything ya do.
You're always mindful to pray before making any move.
And in doing so, you anchor the unfolding —
guided steps and smooth groove.
I'll forever cherish one of the greatest examples you walked in before me:
When I was weary in my "life journey" 'cause circumstances had beat me down,
JESUS in you & Jasmine lifted me up
and I reclaimed the drive to overcome and flourish.
I also was searching desperately for that healing and restoration
of my traumatized emotions and personal development.
And you without judging, condemning, or being overbearing,
just kept praying and encouraging me to go to the place
where you found yours and the gift of relative contentment.

I finally came to my senses and joined you one day.
And ever since, I've received that void's filling.
I've been skipping in my "life journey" in a rejuvenated way.

Thank you so much for bein' so driven, faith-full, therapeutic, and chilled.
You've enriched my life beyond measure;
all that you show then tell; I'll always treasure.

Smooth Glide, Smooth Stride

Been told by my family (on a regular),
"you sure 'nuf walk like your daddy."
And my immediate reaction has always been —
joy exhibited by an ear–to–ear grin.
Why so joy-full? 'cause truly my dad had a calm, cool, and relaxed style.
Just watchin' him — in particular — walking
could make me wallow in observation for a while.
Every now & then I catch my reflection in a mirror on a street;
and I go right to focusing on the glide and stride of my feet.
Every instance takes me back in time to that simple pleasure
of watching my dad make dat move.
Whether walking away or walking toward,
he was a man with a smooth glide, smooth stride.
Thank you, Dad, for passing on that cool part of you to me.
I carry it always with magnified, humble pride.

Spiritual Warfare : Battle-Tested Soldier

Standing firm in the power of His Spirit,
ready for battle to tear down the enemy's strongholds.
Victory will only come as we advance in the attack and remain bold.
There's no room in this army for the wishy washy, the double–minded;
only those who are focused and determined in this crew, will you find 'em.
As we step out in faith and don't allow any hinderances from any distractions,
we'll experience the awesome glory He'll reveal,
it will be so live, so real.
The battle is truly full–fledged warfare, it will be full of vivid and intense activity:
piercing of the Sword in the sides of the enemy's cohorts ;
beating up the esteem of the opposers with God's Word;
praying & worshipping in song and clapping our hands to confuse their concentration;
and finally striking the enemy with singleness of mind, unity, and in–sync orchestration.
Celebrate! Celebrate! Celebrate! It's Time To Celebrate!!!
We have grasped hold of our promised territory —
a portion of God's inheritance to us — laying claim to our fate.

Finally. . .The Kiss

Unexpected, though dreamt about, it happened.
The person of my heart's affection, squared-up and landed it on the lips with perfection.
This longed for kiss set me off, floating high — floating high as the clouds in the sky.
It was too quick, though; didn't get to be caught up in the sweetness of its essence;
desired to wrap myself in its presence.
Do you know what you do to me when we keep company?
Let me tell ya, you have a "bubbling chemistry affect" on me.
The effects: an intense smile, just because daily I think
of you and envision your lovely face;
Wanting to be with you more and more — anytime, anyplace.

Now back to that kiss —
my immediate response as I stood alone was savoring the moment.
Mmm, Mmm.
You drove off and I couldn't wait to tell you later:
It was so special, occurring under a full moon,
you made my dream of it a reality come true.
And now I can't hold it any longer:
"I'm in love with you and can't imagine my life without you."
So, can we take it slow —
Continuin' to solidify our friendship and spend quality time, 2gether?
'Cause it's my hope that our love will abide strong & forever.

Gentle Native Warrior

Short in height, but stood tall.
Feisty and straight up forward, always wuz able to go right to common sense
whenever she spoke.
Believed in being active and livin' life to the fullest,
the more so, the younger she felt.
Naturally had a youthful spirit;
whenever anyone was around her, you gleefully got caught up in it.

My fondest memories were the tea and pastry/ cracker sittings,
hearing my "Muzzie" share about her upbringing on a Native American reservation
and the transition, eventually from the West to the East.
These early years of her life were so special 'cuz they were lived
in traditional Native American style.
Being in-tuned with nature, preserving sacred Mother Earth,
through daily contact with God by prayer, meditation, and dance.
It is due to this paternal matriarch of my family,
who transitioned to eternity in Heaven (Aug. 1986) —
that I will continue to be all of who I am and all of what is mine through my family tree.

Thank you, great–grandma "Muzzie" for living and leaving behind a rich legacy —
you told it well.
And through the generations, I'll encourage the passing on of your story
with humble pride and glory.

My Big Brotha In Christ

In the midst of the congregation after service time,
The Lord found a way to connect us to each other's lives.
And anytime, anywhere following that introduction,
we always greeted each other with open arms, joy with special unction.
What stands out for me, whenever I think of you, is
your cool and genuinely caring demeanor.
Your faith was always reaching for that next upgrade;
you were determined to be the man of GOD that you were called to be,
no allowance to be defeated by the Enemy or your light shine dim to fade.

You were a soldier of service, consistent & diligent when it came to ministry.
Your gift of servanthood you exercised it freely.

You also showed your love to your family (natural & spiritual)
with openness is what I'd always see.
Now, they need that type of love in this time of sorrow.
We who are here can give it — from your example, borrow.

Eddie: I'll love you always;
can't shake the shock that you're gone, and miss you so much!
'Til we fellowship again in eternity, know that my life —
you've significantly touched.

Cool As Ice

Your biography testifies so well, of the power of dreaming and determination.
And by persevering through your hang-ups and obstacles,
your life has become full of highlight sensations.

The Beginning: Ya didn't even give a peep about basketball 'til you wuz 14.
Yet, when ya stepped on the court, your skillz flowed naturally — amazing of sorts.
You realized you liked the game and you were really good at your position.
So, you disciplined yourself and set your 1st goal regarding this game:
earning a scholarship to college.
And upon your high school graduation, you had it —
you were en route to Iowa after thoughtful process.
The plan while at college: to do the academics & basketball to your maximum ability,
no nonsense.
All–American, Pan American Games…the honors rolled on;
one of the most significant — being the 1st University of Iowa female bballer
to have her jersey retired — "that's the bomb."

Lastly, the final stage of the dream — to make it professionally;
and after the footwork, your destination was set for Italy.
There for (9) years and finally the ultimate happened —
the opportunity to continue and finish the career at home.
Now' til you retire, you're "getting off" in the WNBA.
And like Naughty By Nature, your family & friends can directly cheer you on,
"Hey, Ho, Hey!"

I'm so proud of you, sista girl, my friend.
As you continue to be positive, a role model, ya got my support 'til the end.

Promised Companion

"Delight yourself in The Lord and He will give you the desires of your heart."
This is what You say;
and truly, I have seen in my life that this promise pays.
However, there is still one very special desire that I've prayed to happen someday.
The introduction to my "Promised Companion," is that compliment set apart for me;
The One you have as my sweet spice, who will bring glowing glee.

Now let me be clear, Lord —
I'm standing firm in my faith, upholding my single's covenant,
and taking every feasible opportunity to engage in "selective socialbility."
Will the desire become reality?

Through optimism, I'll continue to see —
knowing I have "wonder-fulls" to offer;
and at the appointed time, the desire will actually be.

Feelin' The Beat

Electricity is hovering in the air; Energy is oh so high.
Time to get a groove on is nigh.
And the music plays, settin' off the scene right:
subwoof, thumpin' bass, consuming the place.

Enjoyin' the flava, havin' a swingin' good time with my "G" crew.
We ain't gonna stop 'til we drop,
'til the house closes down and the party is through.

Yeah, we feelin' the beat —
it's phat, it's deep down on the inside, it's all dat.
So, next time you want to be down to feelin' the beat,
remember the only way to do so is to play tunes dat got some fierce heat.

Available & Willing

Encouragement, Giving, Helps, Knowledge, and Teaching —
these are my spiritual gifts, my ministry.
Whether it's through all–around means, Athletes In Action, or my style of poetry.
I am available & willing
To attempt and do what is needed to result in the fulfilling —
the fulfilling of meeting a need,
to view the fruition of a sown seed.
When it concerns a commitment or interest, I strive to keep my word.
When relating one–to–one, I like to mostly listen then,
if able and asked, give good advice.
For me, it's about being a resource that adds spice to life.

Available & Willing —
be an asset versus a liability;
foster peace wherever you are, keep your mind & soul free.

Available & Willing —
Avail your ability; journey on, willingly.
To exhibit your "action power,"
Become a pillar of pure strength, a symbolic refuge tower.

I Am Self–Determined

It was the 5th night of Kwanzaa;
it was the night to celebrate the principle of Nia ("Purpose").
I was asked by one of the co–hosts to represent "Kujichagulia" ("Self–Determination")
—
the 2nd principle of Kwanzaa.
It was a pleasure to do so ; and personally, it's one of my favorite Kwanzaa principles.
And the amplified meaning of "Kujichagulia":
to define ourselves, name ourselves, and speak for ourselves
instead of being defined and spoken for by others.
Yes!!! Amen!!! Word Up!!!

I am self–determined:
seeking through wisdom and resourcefulness to strut with royal ease the originality of me.
I am self–determined:
finding "priceless jewels of ' for your information" about the roots of My Nation.
I am self–determined:
no one or nothing can take away all that I am and have, for real.
I got presence and energy that is attractive for mass appeal.
Yeah, Yeah!!!
It's all good for this native from a Massachusetts urban 'hood.

I Am Self–Determined.
I Am Self–Determined.
I Am Self–Determined!!!
I Am "Kujichagulia" ("Self–Determined")
I Am An Assured African & Native American, "Jehovah Strengthened" Woman;
a Nubian Queen fashioned with beauty, grace, and poise.
Thank you beloved ancestors for all that you invested in our richly, phat legacy.
I Am Self–Determined.
I Am Self–Determined.
I Am Self–Determined!!!
I Am "Kujichagulia" ("Self–Determined")

Ignore The Hype

So much is said when a concert, a celebrity, or otherwise well–advertised event
represents on the local scene.
<u>Caution:</u>
Be careful not to get caught up too quickly.
Sift through the surface buzz, "peep" what's the inside scoop —
so you don't let your mind and energy get trapped in a "hype loop."

Ignore The Hype,
What's the dilly, "straight up," "the right?"
Only "positive players," take heed; don't believe everything you read.
The only real that ya gonna feel,
the only slammin' time that's gonna be sublime;
The only sight that's gonna set your emotions to flight is that which you can claim is mine.

Whatever you place in your space, be certain that you're not flirtin.'
Ignore The Hype —
concentrate solely on all that is genuine and all else will fall in.

Jesus Is In The Houz: Now The Party Is Really On

The faces and soothing, inviting voices of the hospitality ministry —
they're the 1st encounter.
Then, it's your choice as to where to enter the sanctuary and enter in the Inner Sanctum.
Now, time to position yourself in a comfortable, full–effect spot.
Don't want to miss any of the power–packed action,
Ready to cut loose "in the Spirit" during Celebration Service Sundays;
continually seeking to live the Christian life God's way.
Then, there are all of the wonder–full opportunities to be involved in ministry;
take time to identify your passion &purpose and pursue them freely.

Jesus Is In The Houz —
in the church building and in the "ekklesia" ("The Family of God")
Time to accept His Presence in your life, give Him the "yes nod."
You won't be disappointed rather you'll be at the beginning of your "time appointed."

Keep striving to step into "progressive atmosphere shifts,"
the place where your heart, mind, spirit, and soul get an inspired lift.
Go "with the strength" to reach your highest spiritual heights;
Let go and let GOD so that you can take flight.
So, there it is.
Wanna have an amazingly, enriching time in a hot party zone?
Then, enter in where Jesus Is In The Houz, where you're never alone.
From my personal experience,
this is what you got to do to have a guaranteed, lifted time —
remember to arrive early or at least "on time."
Then, just stay open, settle in, and wait for the "party wave" to blow your mind.

The Meaning Of My Name

Michelle Denise Smith —
that's my complete birth name given to me by mi madre,
Ola M. Lumpkin Smith.
My favorite part of my name is the1ˢᵗ —Michelle.
"Michelle" means "Who Is like GOD or Who Is Like The LORD,"
according to the closest Hebrew translation.
And me being a practicing Christian, that meaning is a humbling sensation.

"Denise"—the 2ⁿᵈ part of my name means "Wise Discerner."
Truly, I'm floored by this characteristic gift;
developing and continuously seeking to be my absolute best and through my flaws, sift.

"Smith"—the 3ʳᵈ part and surname;
it's the "family tree root" of my father's side.
I believe it's very important to never dismiss any distinction of who you really are.
Be proud of all that is the all of you, gleam on as does a bright star.
Is "Smith" my true surname or will researching my family history
reveal surprises and mysteries?
Once the family geneology is done, my reflection will be full circle.
'Til then, I am who I am —The Meaning Of My Name.
To better understand and be in touch with yourself,
I encourage you to do the same.

What Ya Gonna Do?

"A double–minded person is unstable in all their ways (James 1:8)."
Are you such a person?
Do you need to make–up your mind about what ya gonna with your days?
What's gonna be the side you choose—your way
or the way that was assigned for you while you were still in your mother's womb?

Win, don't lose. Don't let precious minutes pass by and
miss your calling 'cause you snoozed.
Wake Up !!! Smell the refreshing aroma of some fresh air
and the madd potential of your life yet to come.

You can get there,
if you pay close attention and avoid pride, stubbornness, disobedience, and resistance.
All ya gotta do is stay open, aware, humble, and seek with persistence.
Don't allow complacency or any of those other "ugly detours" camp out.
Ya gotta have a fixation on encountering the wonder of your path's end, no doubt.

The Meaning of My Adopted African Name

Makini Dalila Saada (MDS) —this is my complete, African adopted name
that I chose based on my character qualities.
I know, based on my ethnic roots, that my origin is African of some descent.
Before making the discovery of the source with my African adopted name,
I of course represent wit "the birth right vein."
However, since middle adolescent years, I have always been extremely driven
about knowing the specifics of my genealogy.
Thus, I have been on an ongoing quest; I know my homebase
is one of four parts of Africa, but what part — East, West, North, or South?
Based on my adopted, chosen name, it's East African and Swahili in flava.
Again, I took selections which mirrored my core character qualities and matched
*the abbreviation, **MDS** – Michelle Denise Smith = Makini Dalila Saada.*

And now for the breakdown:
* ❖ *Makini – "Strength of Character"*
* ❖ *Dalila – "Gentle"*
* ❖ *Saada – "Helpful"*

Makini speaks of my ability to withstand adversity — to
overcome by faith and the word of my testimony.
Dalila speaks of my soft, sensitive side.
The way I mingle with folk; I do it with ease and humble pride.
and
Saada speaks of one of my spiritual gifts —"ministry of helps."
I am always willing to do what I can to meet a need.
I don't mind steppin' to the forefront and taking a lead.
And as for my other spiritual gifts —encouragement, giving, knowledge, and teaching
(especially to youngbloods).
Like a rapid, rippling river, I give effort faith–fully & consistently to pour out
all of who I am, have, can does does a flood.

So, there you have it —the meaning of my name.
Here goes a word of encouragement —
claim that which represents you and adopt the same.

My Sistahs

Friendship Is…is one of my personal favorite poems
authored on Oct. 19, 1986.
And it speaks of my opinion about the authenticity
of what friendship should be.
Thankfully, I have exactly what the poems says with my cipher —
and that includes both female and male.
However, there is a certain, special joy that envelopes me
when I ponder the intimate link that I got wit' my sistahs.

My Sistahs. — My Sistahs range in shades of french vanilla and dark chocolate.
My Sistahs have been nourishment to my life from 1976 – Present
and it's been oh so divine;
To what's next for our "sister circle," it's exciting, enriching and oh so fine.
My Sistahs are a mix of many various natural talents, skills, personalities, and styles.
And whenever I'm in their company,
there is a lovely after – effect that just lingers awhile.

Ahh!!! The beauty (inner & outer), energy, and radiance
are wonder-fully complimentary qualities of My Sistahs.
These who I 'm honored & privileged to have in my life's pathway;
I'm gonna cherish and absorb all that we can instill in each other, all our days.

Heaven On Earth

You promised that if I "fight the good fight of faith" and "endured hardness
as a good soldier of Christ," I would receive the harvest of that sowing, an earned prize.
And as you've always proved yourself to be 100% true;
I've always been mindful to give you a proper thank–you.
Yes, Lord!!! Truly, You have blessed me "exceedingly and abundantly
above all that I can ask or imagine;"
and it's only the beginning of a Malachi 3:10 receipt — to me that's absolutely amazing.
I really can't even fathom what the end of this wonder–fully lovely blessing will be.
And that's o.k. 'cause I adamantly am looking forward to the "wait & see."
You'll answer each need and heart's desire with perfect timing —
blocking any & all hinderances by that crafty devil.

Here you go: you asked now just receive.
Just keep doin' what you've been doin', believe.
Like Kirk Franklin & Nu Nation, I'm ready to "Stomp."
Again Lord, thank–you, thank–you, thank–you
for my desired & realized blessings.
Yeah, this is Heaven On Earth!!!
I'm feelin' revived, a deep rebirth.

The Loophole of Plan "A"

Ideas. Plans. Decisions. — We all have them, make them on a regular basis.
However, the outcome doesn't always turn out as we desired in their rightful places.
So, what's up with doing all the necessary footwork;
and then "wham!," unexpected circumstances suddenly cause a setback.
Frustrated when this has happened to me; it made me feel absolutely helpless;
the control that I thought I had decreases to the bottom of less & less.
So, what's the point of making plans at all? —
especially if there is any hint that through the cracks they're gonna fall.
Seriously, what's the point? Hold Up!, this is the solution —
invent a Plan "B" that's bulletproof.
No cracks, no holes, no tensions will be able to, like an explosive,
make it go "kablam! poof!"
Yeah, that's it — When it comes to Plan "B" regarding finances,
the answer is save "mad" loot.
No "robbing Peter to pay Paul" or scrapping 'cause Plan "A" fell through.
I'm determined to be done 'wit' that ;
cuz I've got an inheritance comin' that's gonna situate me financially phat.

When it comes to doin' a social, quality time hangout;
avoid missed rendezvous by owning a mobile phone to relay your delay.
The other option is to reschedule and don't allow anything,
except an emergency, to deter the next connection.
Truly, in all this avoiding the loophole of Plan "A,"
practice will eventually produce a form of protection.

So yes, it's disappointing & frustrating to face dreaded, unexpected circumstances;
the hip knowledge to have, though, is:
Remember when you make plans,
there is always the potential of ripple effects by "physical chances."

W.W.J.D.?

If you're somewhat "in the know,"
you've seen this acronym on bracelets, bumper stickers, and t–shirts.
Do ya know what it means?
It stands for "What Would Jesus Do?
It's meant to be a reminder of how to respond to situations and interactions.
For me, W.W.J.D.? is not just a symbolic inscription;
rather, it's a mindset that is present in every intention.

W.W.J.D.? is a daily, moment–by–moment rubric
of fortifying my evolving, personal development.
And I take extreme seriousness in protecting it with gentle sentiment.

Yeah, W.W.J.D.? —an enriching & residual benefit
each time that I do it right.
Gonna remain adamant about keeping the habit tight.

Forthcoming Publications
By: M.D. Smith

- ❖ *Positioned and Blessed* © 2000
- ❖ *Next Steps, New Heights* © 2003
- ❖ *New Beginnings* © 2005
- ❖ *"8 Points of True Success: A Motivational Speaking Presentation"* © 2006

Final Note

If you enjoyed any segment of this book and/or have any questions or thoughts,
please share with me

_or_

If you are affiliated with a non–profit organization and would like to use this book
as a fundraising tool and keep 100% of the proceeds,
contact me
@
mdsmith@MissionPossibleCollaborative.com.